A

GRAND

WALTZ

Written and edited by:

Derick San Jose

ISBN-10: 1718647948

ISBN-13: 978-1718647947

www.dearpoet.com

To My Readers,

I will always be forever thankful for the ones that supported me throughout this magnificent and unforgettable venture of authoring this book. I will never find the right words to express my gratitude towards your unending support. I hope this book takes you to places you've never been as it did with me whilst taking on this wonderful journey.

From the very bottom of my heart, thank you.

Yours truly,

Derick San Jose

TABLE OF CONTENTS

D. E. A. R. P. O. E. T. II

F. I. V. E. S. E. V. E. N. F. I. V. E. (and shorts) IV

F. O. U. R. S. E. A. S. O. N. S. V

D. A. Y. D. R. E. A. M.

Daydream,

I see the Angel smile to me

and so came along a blissful of glee—

such a beautiful day.

Daydream,

I dreamt about the daisy flowers

and they blossomed every hour

as she walked through the fields.

Marigold

There was once, as sure as time—
a beautiful paradise, perfect for mine.
A sweet scent of the glowing flower
had come by that no man could have ever defied.
I grasped upon that glamorous grandeur—
for it was the Marigold I longed for.

Now there is time, not sure as once.
How could have I lost
my once perfect paradise.
Have I claimed and not embossed?
Or have I blatantly thought about the
abeyance—that I long to disappear.

My once glamorous grandeur,
I long for your bliss—
the sweetest aroma—
my Marigold.

Only Cupid Can Declare

The Sun rays its light upon her
Indeed I was bedazzled.
The radiant smile she bears—
It makes me want to build her a castle.
"Would you like to go with me" I asked.
But she said, "Only Cupid can declare."

The Sun is falling yet she shines through.
Indeed, it was dark but she was a glamorous glimmer.
The Moon gazed and floated over the barrow
for Cupid declared us to share—
quoth, "a still love, comes my arrow."

Retrouvailles

From the Sun on out
and the daylight twinkling to dusk,
I will wait.

From the eve on out
and the stars blinded by your eyes,
I will stay.

And the rest of the universe
will revolve around us, waiting for two lovers
to fall again.

And finally the sky
will be brightened by the smiles of two lovers—
retrouvailles—and our hearts recover.

An Endeavor

I strive, I seek, and I will even
sail the Seven Seas.
Drained and dreaded—
I am set to give in.
But I will walk a million miles more for that
one special kiss—
because to find you is my endeavor,
my dearest queen.

Honey

Cover me in your sweetness—
a kiss or two
and
I will let you fall in my sweet caress.
Your eyes,
the sweetest chocolate-drop eyes,
they certainly put me in
a candyland.
You are the sweetest dessert—
a honey.

Her Lips and Mine

Her lips and mine
must be a dream;
all I desire is a kiss
even if the stars do not align.
To love and have her in my grasp
even if the Moon refuses to form
a tide with the ocean
or to hold her hands
in a form of slow-dance;
the two of us together—
moonstruck in each other's gaze.
Thus our worries will drift away
and her lips and mine can kiss
for forever and a day.

For We Kissed the Kiss

For we kissed the kiss,
our journey begins quite
in a bliss.
After a long endurance,
I took your lips—
three soft words spoken
for assurance;
came from the heart within.
I, staring at your eyes
as I held your chin.
It was there and then,
for when we kissed the kiss.

Heavenly

Take this celestial rose
and I will be forever yours.
I see your halo glow;
I will follow it and never be lost.
With you, I can escape these woes and sorrows.
Thus I sing of an angel
flying me away from the frost.

Even the Angels

Those red lips of yours—
so tender
and your rosy cheeks
I always ponder.
In between this starry hour,
even these flying angels
watch in fervor.

Celestial Angel

To fall deep in her gaze
and all of her celestial beauty,
Heaven dawned for an Earth Angel
insatiable for a romance so free.
Her crimson lips craving—longing
for a gentle kiss I could fly across the sea.
And those mesmerizing eyes,
her chocolate-drop eyes,
          the ones to intoxicate a man...
                    ...reflecting her heartbeat so fine.

The Break of Dawn

There came a ray of the dimmed Sun
but came to appear so splendidly bright.
To shine it did though discretion
must dawn in our might.
The eve has ran far away
but the two of us bounded to stay.
And she clung her body to mine
with her voice so soothing.
The dash of these gazing lights
moved so swiftly to her radiant smile—
as it was our desire to romance
until the break of dawn.

Honey

Cupid, send her ways to a courtly love.
I come unto you with a rose or two
o' send her to my way and
all of my dreams will finally fall in place.
My sweet, sensuous honey,
my valentine—you are the one.
Cover me with your dainty kisses,
dip me in your sweet caress.

Cotton Candy

Her words are so delicate
and her whispers makes
these butterflies inside entwine.
Her gaze is so intricate
and two endearing hearts form and align.
Her love is so exquisite
and her world is o' so fine.

Her Castle

Beneath the shadow over a swing—
a true fidelity in her own heart
as if she was her own queen.
And as she is swinging by,
her castle caught a glimpse
of her colorful smile—
lilac flowers and starry skies
and rainbows and pretty clouds;
she glances and dances and sees
that she is in love for a while.

Dream of Me

Dreamy damsel, will you dream of me?
The starry sky shimmers in sheer sanctity
whenever we weave around in glee.
A world where we will stargaze at night—
a world where our love lingers
around us endlessly.
And there we are, as we were,
floating in the marmalade sky,
holding hands for assurance
and your soft lips on mine.
You and I in a bliss—
dreamy damsel, are we still in a dream?

For Her

I am falling for her.
She is captivating—
an angel in disguise.
Her heart is so pure—
she is benevolent.
My heart beats for
the right reasons now.
I'm falling,
            I'm falling,
                        I'm falling.
Falling deeply for the right reasons.

Chinita

Red, cherried-lips
I could taste just from looking.
Your little, cheeky smiles captured
my dreams and made it theirs.
When those little chinita eyes meet mine,
they tell me to never look away—
they ask for your cherry lips to fall on mine,
"o' they are so addicting," they say.
Dear, reel me in,
pull me closer,
I wish to be
loved by you.
Dear, hold my hand,
I'll grasp onto yours,
I wish to have a lifetime with you.
Dear me, I have fallen for you.

Her Oceans

My roses float over your shallow oceans
and they ask for you, my paramour.
Come unto me and your waters will never wither—
waves shall form and soon
your maroon lips will meet mine.
Grasp on these bed sheets
whispers echoing in my ears.
Let us be until it is only you
I can call home.

To Catch a Butterfly

Running freely beneath the marmalade sky,
it is us chasing these butterflies inside us.
It is soaring up high,
reaching for our fairy tales that
we long to be a part of.
Longing to be set free and
so long to our heartaches,
it is us flying like these butterflies.

Something About Her

Something in the way she glows
reminds me of the beauty
of God's wonderful creations.
Something in her smile she shows
entraps the being of mine
in an endearing daydream.
I can see the fairy tales
I longed for in her eyes
because something in the way she is
enchants me like a daydream—
the most endearing one.

Renewing Vows

I could stare at you forever—
your glittering eyes are
just like the sparkling stars—
magnificent glamour.
I cannot help but think,
how splendid our love can be—
you're the one worth fighting for.
And I, your chivalrous knight,
a noble man who will always be
by your side;
your story hero—
silently serenading you in the night.
Thus us romancing forevermore.

Fairy Tale

I see stars in you—
so soothing in my eyes.
I ought, just once,
for this night to stay—
'o so bright, Serapia.
Thus I can show you
this fairy tale I always dream—
of the truest love with you
I long to be.

Our Romance

A candor of two—
spoken from within;
a perpetual pledge that
came before our love
for a promise that will
never go rue.
True love holds the two—
and three heartfelt words
were spoken so dearly—
for love went about between the two.

For All Time

Hold my hand and grasp it tight,
call the angels and they will sing of love.
It is you I desire the most,
it is you I wish for day and night,
It is you I will love with all my might.
Call the angels and let them sing
of our romantic nights.
The harmonies will linger on until the end of time—
you and I will listen to them for all of time.

The Way You Love Me

There you are,
as perfect as you can be.
Into a gazing sun
and you shine so perfectly.
Through my vows,
I promise to grasp on you for eternity.
Say that you love me
and my whole world will be certainly free.

Forever So

The ocean so blue
and only her and the stars
can find me in the darkness.
When everything else falls
and there is no moon to brighten up the night.
Maybe the Sun will refuse to shine and never dawn.
But when she says those three words
spoken from within,
I can also love her...forever so.

Under the Stars

For all of my life
I yearned for a kiss that will capture my dreams.
Dreams of mine that you will set free
with your luscious lips and rainbow smile.
To fall in love in the blink of an eye,
only moments have passed and I have fallen for you.
As your lips touched mine,
she yearned for a love so true.
In her eyes, I was her dream—
milky-chocolate eyes and daydream smile.
She cannot fathom the fragrance of a love so divine.
"Look no further and lay it all on me.
Let's seek the most innocent love we could ever have.
Leave your worries and troubles away
and I will do so as well.
Let us be young and love until daylight.
It will be the two of us
making love under the stars."

Pillowtalk

Is this magic in your eyes
or am I dreaming?
We can make it through the night
and our love will dawn.
Come unto the stars—
your castle has been waiting.
"Lock me in your arms,
still moonstruck by your eyes.
Lock your arms in mine,
bring the stars
and
put me in a daze,"
she declares.

A Wondrous Paramour

The beauty of romance never ceases,
with you I bound to be forever.
A chalice that will never empty
never to yearn again—
you are where I long to be.
Stay, sway,
never lead me astray, ever.
Let the flowers be envious of your sweet scent
for it is a glamorous grandeur I cannot defy.
A forever lasting bond to be with you—
a wondrous paramour in my own eyes.

D. E. A. R. P. O. E. T.

It must be nice
to write in glee,
to write as if you were free;
waltzing in between memories—
inking the Poet's mind and
living in an induced dream.

To wake as if they were true;
the ballads, the fairytales, the sonnets...
the mere, wondrous creations
where we allow ourselves
to compose a classical symphony
or paint a picturesque masterpiece.

The art of a poet's dream
where it yearns to compose not
a monotonous symphony
or paint a grotesque memory.
Often a poet dreams
and it will scrawl a poetry so enchanting.

Lily, the Moon Seeks Rest

i
The moon sought rest and
the water splashed through her pale skin
as she danced and danced danced—
in the like amidst the dawn.
But the moon sought rest—
and so he asked, "Lily of the Lake,
shall we dare call the Sun?"
The marmalade sky appeared
and so did the beauty of the clouds
for we danced and danced and danced.

ii
The moon said farewell
and so the deep ocean sank—
a beauty in disguise she appeared to be.
"Lily, now the moon is resting,
and the bright star burning,
I ought to continue
my august romance with you," he declared.
And so she replied, "my dearest, my dearest,
let us rest as we wait for our moon."
Thus their romance continued
Like how the Sun waits for the moon,
day and night—
searching tirelessly—
eternally.

Win

A step into the wild
with no serenity in the heart.
An armageddon in the mind
between still and change;
afraid or brave.
Be still thyself and win—
soon you will meet
the rainbows after this daunting rain
and it will greet you with warmth
over a sky free of rainy clouds.

The Tragedy in Antioch

The dawning sky blew up and
the starry night appeared.
Have the Heavens opened up for her?
Her splendid smile seemingly seeped
through the heart of a broken man.
"O' Serapia of Antioch, come unto me,
with you, I vow to love once more,"
the broken man said.
But he dared unconvincingly—
a broken man he is—
and the Heavens did not wait.

The Story of Everybody

No moon, no stars
can understand the torture
inside my head—
my own agonized universe.

The Art of Silence

Once upon a piteous noon
comes a ponderous, paper-thin,
morose man, a goon.
Pardon my rudeness, I pity
such gleeful gestures—so gloom.
"'Tis picturesque borough," I murmured.
And more cunning with Serapia,
my wondrous paramour.
Such affection wretches
unto this art of silence—
need no apologies—petty mime!
Your dance plagues my damning eyes!

<u>Claudia</u>

The coronation of Claudia has begun!
(Exit Esquire)

Crown be thine (Enter Claudia)
Of the shrine
Less be gone.
The clouds still hang
Daytime, where is the Sun.
But the throne hath purge—
Gone in grief, I suppose.
Impotent, I am
For love cannot
Behold no longer.
Out of the castle
And lost meticulously forever.

A Dainty, Young Lady Slapped Me

A dainty young lady walks so keenly
and her dapper self, o' so pretty.
She wears talc over her rosy cheeks
and a red stain will soon cover my soft lips.
Her British accent—so prestigiously gorgeous.
A dainty, young lady walks in front of me
and I see that she is a model of her own fashion.
A chat she holds but
"My apologies, dearest Madame,
a kiss or two—o' so passionately, please?"
And she grabs my head,
and all happening so swiftly—
"My first ever kiss," I blur.
And a red stain covers my reddening cheeks.

Damsels and Daffodils

Dearest, blue I am.
Mas I ask for your name?—
No, along the way I will.
"Dear damsel, daffodils?"
Violin, viola, cello!
"The daffodils are so yellow,"
she smiled sunnily.
Alas, we strode along
the hall whilst waltzing—
surprising?
Had I asked for her name?—
No, along the way I found.

Waltz for Two

The sunset so warm
in this classic ball—
ah, the masquerades
so frighteningly beautiful.
A jazz so soothing
and our dance begins.
Step one and step two
and our feet flows so cool.
"Take my hand, Talïa,
I am keen to waltz you until
the light of day," I said.
Quoth her, "only if you give me
the star I have been looking for
in the night, I will."

Slow Dance

Thereabouts on a sunny day
and these weeping clouds are running away.
The Sun took its light upon her
and now she is radiating like the daisy flower.
She is the girl in the white—
appearing to be so splendidly bright.
And there we stood, longing for a smile.
"Would you take my hand for a dance," I asked.
For she said, "only in a form of slow-dance."

Butterflies

I hear the butterflies inside
as they weave my heart around.
So I hummed along with them
and dearest, they were dancing for you.
Hence the soft music slowly
turning into a crescendo—
you wearing that splendid smile—
a waltz for us two.

Let Us Dance

May I have this dance—
I will sing of adoration.
Dear, let me hold you under this chilling sky—
let us free love from our endearing hearts.
Let us dance between the stars and
we will sing of romance—
less we sought and
have fate take its course.
My muse, my wondrous paramour,
my forever treasure on the dance floor.
Dearest, let us waltz forever.

A Grand Waltz

Twinkling and tinkling
beneath the grandest stars,
she expresses her love
through our celestial dance.
A definite angel in my own eyes—
I am in awe as
she danced
          and danced
                    and danced
to the angels' harps.
A Heaven sent in her splendid smile—
a cunning one that will forever stay in my heart—
and a grand waltz waiting for us two.

Fruits, Hopes, and Lemons

Darling, do be sincere
and accept our fate.
Two hearts disappeared
and now true love can wait.
All can happen in a sudden bliss
and o' it shall never perish—
soon you will find your royal kiss.
Do keep dreaming on, my dearest.
Hold on until there is only
desire in your eyes—
but that is the trouble with hope, Honey;
it is too hard to resist.

The Cry

i
Tell me your desires and I'll fulfill them twice.
No—I promise you, I'll do them always.
I lost you once for that I regret.
But now I'm a better man—
for you, I've changed.
I vow to be your prince once again—
I'm ready to start anew.
"So take my hand Maria, isn't this what you want?" I said.
And so she replied, "My dearest one, put me out of this blue
and waltz with me for I've missed you dearly."—
thus begin my dream, once again.

ii
As time molds and
a day cannot go by—
what if our plans go awry?
I've longed to tell you
what meddles me astray.
Comes a day when you will
push me away.
Maria, I lost you once
for that I regret,
I've come to change—
I'm frightened you might leave again.
The dream might not endure.

The Artist

The sunset so dim
and on my east comes
the artist so keen.
A girl, brunette—
readily holds her pencil
as I glared—
into the dawning nightfall.
An endearing scene that had caught her attention—
for it is inevitable for an artist
to draw with emotion—
so scenic.

The Pleasurer

Sir, it is I, "with you" for the night.
I wear this mask and behind
you must not see.
Ponder not for I am "not" writhing
in despair.
Beneath this mask you are not to see—
I am simply in "glee."
Sir, I am the dancer of the night;
a pleasure to you.

Goodnight

Goodnight, Princess.
I have met my Queen.
Dancing across your castle and
I yearned to be your story hero.
But times change and so did the heart of mine.
There goes my queen, looking so fine—
she is among the most endearing one.

The Love Within

There was once, as sure as time,
a love—no, a folly, so untrue;
full of tumultuous clamors as told.
"Do us a favor and elope with me," he said.
But she replied, "Dear—I shall forsake
you and our love shall perish."
Thus, he was dethroned by his own queen—
a damsel in distress never found love within.
Need not pity—
his merriment was long gone;
he lurks for damsels for dowries.

Madame

A night so cold
and the river never flows.
The weary town so bright
but she could never see the dark.
The ticking hour of delight—
and hears the people's excitement.
But she is drowned by her tears,
waiting for someone to put her out of despair
and give her the diamond—
a joy that can last forever
and a lust that can shine in the dark.

Your Troubadour

Here I am waiting for you—
your yearning troubadour.
For I am here, allow me in,
Mademoiselle—
"Une femme de l'amour,"
Let me write to you;
to show you the grand beauty
you bestow upon this damning world.
May I take those lily-like lips of yours—
a sweet aroma in my heart.
Let me touch those lips with mine—
as a gratitude for our declaration of love,
my dear Madame.

Cino

Cino passed by her today—
she seemed rueful.
A jewel in the sea she was—
a rare beauty in its possession.
She may have been his once,
a glamorous gem—
for which Cino have vowed to
treasure until such—
grasping upon the earnest
Pearl of the Great Sea.

Eldiron of Roma—The Lone Fisherman

The Aegean Sea growled in anger
And to the Gods
He begged insignificantly—
"Spare me not and dare put your wrath in me!"
Said Eldiron of Roma—
A lone fisherman.

I Am Dreary, Succubus

Seep in as I sleep, Lady in White.
Lure me in a lucid dream
and hallucinate me with your Hell on fire.
I have succumbed to you, Succubus.
It seems as though I can never make peace with You;
coming into terms with your tormented soul.

Cinderella

It has been past winter—
yet it is still cold.
Yes, in my heart, it is still aching—
even the slightest fire frosts.
I have molded this world
to make a better castle for you.
But where have you been?
I have not seen a sight of you—
Have we already part?
I pray you still possess my own heart.
"You're tattooed on my mind,
Cinderella, how can you let go?
Didn't you promise me a love forever
true?" I cried.
She did not come—
and so I strode along the cold eve,
longing for the promise I hope
she still holds.

A Story of Old Times

A story of old time and says
he was afraid of their journey
that have been long sought.
"Come so many years' a blank
and I fear our plans might fall apart," he said.
But she replied, "Although these unwritten
words we cannot seek,
the journey we have is enough
for me to think, that I will be yours,
surely forever."

To Eleanor

Dear Eleanor,
have you not loved me enough
for you to say—and quoth you, "nevermore."
The prince that you molded in me—
Eleanor, I desired for a princess in you;
you cheated me with words and
for that I am baffled with understanding—
of how a perfect love in my eyes
was just an illusion for my blind heart.

He Promised

You promised me a wedding ring
and have me as your beauteous bride.
But here I am standing at the altar,
wearing black instead of a silky-white gown.
You promised me you would never leave—
you could have told the angels, simply "no."
But here I stand at the altar,
wishing I could hold your hand
while you say your vows.
Thus I could be your perfect princess—
crying of joy and not of mourn.

The Ballerina: Artists & Poets

She could not dance properly—
what was wrong with her?
She was once the ballerina
that quite frankly showed emotions—
through her fluid movement.
Is she content?
Has she found her way?—
pursuit to happiness.
What is thou art without agony and compassion?
For, which, every artists & poets
sincerely suffer from.

The Clock

The clock strikes Twelve
And here it is, the last farewell.
Demurred and demised,
still I dwell on until "Adieu!" to myself.
Through time's ticking clock, hear the bells
Ring as I bid thee farewell.
Once midnight, I can begin anew;
Wearied but a warrior, I, too, can now sleep
And by morning I will feel the breeze
and the cold dew.
To my dearest star, my watcher's keep,
I ought to burn a Sun 'til we seek togetherness
for a while.
And as time goes by,
I will remain the same and that I can admire;
all will be a haze wearing but a different face.

For I Am A Poet

Tell me what meddles you;
show me your world and
I'll ponder a classic—
I can write you away.
Allow me to capture your thoughts
and let me fill your emptiness
with these words I dare to compose.
For I am a poet,
take my hand and I'll write you away.
For it is my duty to persuade you back to your place.
So allow me to fulfill your way—
for you to claim your chase.
I will write to you and I promise to until
we meet the day—
for I am the poet.

A. S. T. R. A. L. S.
&
S. T. E. L. L. A. R. S.

Vega, Eris,

shine no more.

Her light is enough for me

to see my world turn into

the brightest in the universe.

Stargazing

The eve—the moon sing to us
as the stars echo our romantic song.
Whenever she is near to me,
a symphony whispers so close into my ears
as we stargaze in each other's eyes.

"Let us sing with them;
these bright lanterns are so inducing—
I ought to sing the night with you," she said.

For then and there we fell in love—
stargazing in each other's eyes
and in amongst the billions of stars
glowing in the singing sky above;
she is the only one to sing so beautifully in my heart.

Meteor Rain

The fire in a roar to keep us close
and the cold in a chilling craze
to keep us near and away from the frost.
Even the birds sing in harmony
in hopes the we can dance
while the moon illuminates
our most endearing night.
And my dreamiest dream came true—
waiting for the stars to fall on us
as she lay on me waiting for a sudden kiss.
Two hearts beating for one,
in sync and in love,
a picturesque scene bound for one
to fall for the other.
And the whole world falls in love
as we dance our first dance.
Thus the stars begin to rain upon us
as two lips meet in a sudden bliss.

Stars & Diamonds

Lead me to the stars
and be my diamond.
This empty universe yearns for a glistening kiss.
Lead me to the stars
as they glow in the beat of a heart.
And as you hold my hand closer
the stars align and gleams stronger.
Let our love prove its truest fidelity.

Meteor Shower

I look into your eyes
and dare I say I am sane.
With your raining stars
brightening up my night.
With you my whole universe
is at ease.
With you, there is forever.

Luminosity

The light was nowhere to be seen,
the sunshine was in haze
and the world was dimmed.
He reaches from afar
as he gazes in pleasure.
Though the lady in teal, twinkling in twilight—
she was seen sparkling, shimmering
like a star in a dark sky.
Seen only by the man, from afar,
looking for a speck of light—
it was her, he found in the quiet world.
"You are so close in my grasp
but you still seem distant," she said.
To which he replied, "let your glow shine
until you have light up my way.
Let it glow until you become my sunshine, I pray."

Moondance

It was him and her in a dance
that even the moon refused to come up —
he found his sunshine within her eyes.
"Count the stars
until they gleam no longer," he said.
"Count them until you are the only one
to shine across the sky."

<u>Summer Nights</u>

We romanced over a spring moon
in a salacious, summer night.
The stars saw us descent from
the colored crescents of the sky—
need we rest darling,
we have been dancing on
our wings since daylight.
"All is well, dearest.
I still see the universe in your eyes," she says.

Starship

I will follow the river
until the stars themselves align
to guide my way to her galaxy
I will walk the stars
until they burn no longer
and so begins my venture to her universe.
She is my only endeavor—
my absolute treasure.

Written in the Stars

Under the gleaming Sun,
tears continued to flow
as you compose so ravishingly beautiful.
Your tears flowed through
the silent heart of mine
and there you sat,
so lonely—so sad.
An angelic face beneath
those crystal eyes
weeping from the cracks
and demise of your precarious romance.
An eloquent diary written
under the stars—
and I, could not bear
but to read and quoth you,
"in my desires for a romance
that will never go rue."

See Her

See her dance under the stars,
bathing in the moonlight.
See her smile and over with her cry.
See the serendipity in her eyes
and the serenity in her heart.
See her fall in love at ease
beneath the brightest moon.
See the rivers and oceans and tides,
the Heaven and the sky—
see the universe fall in her grasp
for she is a Goddess in love.

Yin and Yang

Every morning for you was
when the Sun called Luna
for my night to follow.
Every little stars revolved around us
but we always eclipsed and never met in the middle.
My love, my agony—
my beautiful memory.
"Call for the stars and fly through
the depths of space," she said,
"meet me halfway and Dearest our love will be forever true."

Much Too Soon

What I have with you
a devotion so dazzling—
we declared our love not to go rue.
"Take my hand and shall
we lie beneath the stars," I asked.
But she said, "though we may lie upon
the Moon so blue, maybe this is much too soon."

<u>Supernova</u>

Places I can't go
for something is holding me back.
Memories flow around
and explode like a supernova.
Escaping from a desolated palace
and hiding away from the Sun.
But unlike the common star,
you were the one that burned brighter,
the darkest star and like a black hole—
I try to push away but end up falling again for you.

<u>The Diamond and the Stars</u>

i

As I scrawl in the deepest pit of our romance,
for forty moons and many years,
I have not a sight of you.
Holding onto your promise
and to have you whisper it in my ears,
quoth you, "to love you is like loving
the Sun—so amusing, so grand."
Comes a day—today
and I see you waltzing
with another man.
O', I writhe in agony—
may this end in a good memory.
But dearest, why marry the diamond
when you were in love with the stars?

ii

To love you is like loving the Sun—
so amusing, so grand,
yet so far away, so distant.
Romancing in between the sky and above,
and by night you are long gone.
Indeed I admire the stars
but darling, you never expect
the Sun to love you back!
Ah—you brought the stars together
yet you fell through.
To love you was like the Sun—
so amusing, so far, so grand, so distant.
Tell me, dear, could I have waited
for countless days and o' for so many nights
I prayed that you would put me in
a glow once you have come to shine.
And I thought—the Sun itself will
never refuse to shine
but here we are,
weaving among the stars
and as we were,
never gleaming after dusk.
Enough with time,
an intricate diamond reflects a light
and it glistens just like the stars—
and it promised to ne'er chisel away.

F. I. V. E.

S. E. V. E. N.

F. I. V. E.

(and shorts)

Something troubles me.

Why can't I write properly?

I am the poet.

Good Old-Fashioned Lover Boy

Let me serenade
in gentle ways, Mademoiselle.
I can sing the songs.

Warmth

I feel sunnily
in the amidst of winter
for your love warms me.

One Too Many Faces

Oblivious you are!
Here you are—vulnerable!
Learn to wear faces!

The Moonlight

Set the stars apart.
Seek the light of the night and
bathe on the moonlight.

Of Her & His Concern

Have we gone awry?
Because I often see you
beyond the far cry.

The Forgiven

Her tears dropped slowly.
And on this situation
she, then, took my hand.

Lost

We were lost lovers:
The "forever and a day"
romance we both sought.

Searching

Only to be found
in the rain we were both in,
seeking for warmth—love.

Lovers

I'm in love again—
she's an ethereal sunshine
dawning in the sky.

Sunflower

The Sun kissed her skin
and now she radiates just
like a sunflower.

Let's Wait

Dear, elope with me—
the night is certainly free.
"Maybe we can wait."

Always

"How could I forget?
You're still written in my heart,"
he tearfully plead.

Her Veil

She took off her veil
as she found out he wasn't
the prince she once knew.

She kept a long list
of many broken hearted.
She was one of them.

Her veil was white-silk.
Although drenched for her sorrow—
she wished to subside.

The Devils in Me

Whenever she is near to me
my devils turn against their beliefs
and knock on the gates of heaven.

The Goddess

A sunless day covered in clouds,
I am struck by your gaze as your
eyes caught mine—
slowly unveiling my heart's shroud.

Besançon

Lost angel why come unto thee?
'Tis love will meet the end—
c'est la vie, Ange!
- A word from Cupid from
a heartbroken in Besançon.

Unrequited

She's dreamy.
She's clearly
in love with the sight of him.
I'm weary.
I'm dreary
that she could not see that within me.

Requiem

Fear me—do not love me.
Fear me—I can drag you to my hell
Kiss me—do not leave me.
Kiss me—I can see my soul escaping
Free me—free me.

Storm

Cleanse your broken soul
as you rain viciously.
Your life has seen nothing but storm—
calmly chase the clouds away.

The Rainbow

And the saddest soul sang,
"there is a rainbow always after the rain!"
in hopes to bury the memories
that made him weary.

If You Can

Three words spoken from within;
ardently, earnestly, and fervidly—
"catch my dreams."

Chess

No I'm not asking for forgiveness
it has taken its part.
Leave me and never return
was your game,
and I was the pawn you played.

The Voices in My Head

The voices in my head
call on me and say they never lie.
Can I trust them or am I talking to myself to get by?
They keep saying you'll come back to me
and all will be fine—
the voices in my head.

Bottle of Smoke

She aims to let go
and wander around a world full of her desires—
a gate out of a fictitious life.
Like a smoke in a bottle,
opening up is her only way to escape.

Still Singing

Ten thousand moons have passed
since I last saw you.
But here I am spending the night,
thinking about you.
Every pulsating light comes from afar—
I still wish to it like a shooting star.
Here I am still singing for the one I loved for a while.

F. O. U. R.

S. E. A. S. O. N. S.

Just you and I

under this April Sky—

Marmalade and Peach.

When it gets cold in this

chilling craze,

you hold my hand

and

we embrace...

...this is a rain I don't mind.

It's Autumn, Dear

Dearest, it's autumn.
The leaves are falling,
it is dying—the blossom.
Come away with me, darling.
I ought to see out of the gloom—
why must spring come so far
and the summer warmth longing to stay.
Take my hand—
for my warmth will make its way
to the frosts that meddles you—
it's almost winter, my dear.
Allow me to fulfill your desires—
for dearest, it's autumn.

Winter Solstice

It is the solstice of winter, Dearest.
With you, I gasp for more warmth—
for this cold meddles me.
"Dare I say more, with you
I am bound to love more," she said.
Ah, spring—summer seems so sincere.

Cast A Forever

Can we be the love birds
for they sing happily in the
morning meadows—
a shooting star in the twinkling night
for it bears the endless dreams and promises.
Cast me a forever
and promise me to never let go.
And as our days come in fervor,
the dreams we see could be so
our joy.

Southern Sky

A glam she is and
a flourishing flower always bloom.
Her smile brings
the Sun of the southern sky,
and endearing one, too.
A love so deserved —
for a glam she is.

The Rain & the Sun

The rain and the Sun—
they sigh out of love.
A comfort may come
in a form of slow dance—
a glimmering ray of light touches gently
as the rain dances with the Sun.

A Rainy Day

Once upon a rainy day,
there she sat,
so lonely, so sad.
A beat of a heart
in cadence with the pouring rain.
"O' these mellow clouds have been covering the sky for too long.
Suddenly your storms seem to seep into my sorrows," she cried.

Summer Sky

Her smile lit up the sky
And she kept the promise
Of forever—togetherness.
She brought the Sun out of the wintry wake
And we have been chasing the clouds away.

<u>The Grey Sky</u>

The sky so grey though
it has been past winter.
Loneliness—why plague
the heart with such distress—
for it is spring and the
flowers should have bloomed.
Why—she brought happiness
though her romance left me vexed
and the loneliness still persists.

The Blue Sky

Wind, blow my worries away—
to be gone with you and moreso on my sorrows,
will it take an eternity to escape the currents?
A sky this blue yearns for her canvas to be colored.
Let it be of beautiful colors—
it seems as though my life will be in color.

Summer Daydream

A day so cold will soon shift
in its hot, summery day—
will she gladly take me as I welcome her
with the warmest embrace?
It must be nice to be back in her arms
as I dream away.

Waiting For the Rain

Hear the clouds as they roar somewhere faraway.
Gone in grief and lost in the sky,
where is the rain when I need it the most?
I have kept these tears for too long.
Alas it is time they fall
and here I am, longing for rainfall.

Of One's Last Kiss - A Letter

Have the Heavens parted its way?
Or have we had the slightest clue?—
of problems with such array.
If you did, you could have told me—
why must you not feel so rue?
It has been since winter
but the cold still lingers
in this cloudless summer.

Warmth

They told me to seek warmth,
So I did.
They told me to seek light,
So I did.
They told me to seek joy,
And so I did.
But they never told me she would leave.
And now I gasp for her warmth, light—
all of my joy.

Mote of Light

Winter never stopped—
the striding winds walked wearily
in this darkness that consumed me.
Until she came, I was no gentry
but a mote of light seeking for
a gentle warmth.

Her Winter

The trees whispered air
and I was gladdened.
Though this air bear the cold
and I find myself saddened.
"Let the frosts out of me,
I beg I beg," I said.
But she has already found
her summer in someone else.

Dispel

The crying world felt empty
and the Sun gloomed in the shadow.
The flowers gasped for no pity
and the endless sorrow
never left the sobbing meadows.
"Serapia, I wish to be yours again,
for I cannot dispel our love," he said,
"I always dreamed that you never
intended to undo our love."

It's Cloudy In My Head

My thoughts are clouded
will I be fine in the morning?
It is raining inside my head—
typhoons and monsoons
storm me in.
I'm chained
I can't break free
I'm shackled into this lingering dejection.
release me,
unchain me,
redeem me.

Breathe
slowly
and
win.

U. N. S. E. N. T.

L. E. T. T. E. R. S.

If you're reading this:

I miss you, I'll always love you, and I'm sorry.

I hope you are doing amazing things,

and I hope you know I think about you every day.

Unsent Letters

Tears staining your letters,
distress dripping down,
and drowning my happiness away.
A rush heartbeat that keep on knocking,
will you please open the door...
my heart is crying.
I am locked out of your castle
and lost meticulously forever.

Sorrow

As I scrawl in sorrow
the awe of lust and romance
bruise me in despair—
down I go into abyss.
Thoughts about the love I had with you
and here I ponder—
what does he possess that you
can never see in me?

Photograph

It sat inside my wallet,
the photograph of us.
The color, the hue, the happiness—
they blissed away so sudden.
"How long will your love last," I asked.
She replied, "until the last breath
of color fades away."

To My Dearest

Through this endless nightmare,
it is the agony I cannot bear.
You promised me in secret
that it is your love I will never regret.
I gave you all my might
and for a time you were my light,
but Dearest I now possess this broken heart.
Woe unto me though I still pray—
because you promised me that you will be there.
To promise a forever in hopes
that you will never forget—
Dearest, I have gone through
a cold winter without your soothing warmth.
Until there is light to reflect
against these dark shadows,
it is your sunshine I will hold onto
and never will I cower.

Strangers

You were invisible to my eyes
on the days I needed you the most.
These days are passing by and
I have yet to realize what we once
had are now lost.
And every time I have
the urge to talk to you,
it hurts me to think that
we are just strangers.
You have let go of me.
You don't want me talking to you.
You don't want me to be a part of your life...
like I never existed to you.

The Calling

i
If you stay on my mind,
all of me will falter.
Having you out of my thoughts
every little bit of me was turned over.
I hate your love,
I quench your love,
I hate the fact that I cannot live
without you by my side.
If this was our last time together,
why do I still dream on?

ii
What's it like on the other side—
are you happier...sadder than me?
Like a rope we hold onto this mutual feeling we had,
I tried to burn it but I realized soon
it will take me with it.
I want to know of the other end,
the other side—
how are you, did you let go?
Did you hate me that much
that you never bothered to say hello?
If you stay on my mind…
…all of me will falter.

Kryptonite

Why do I even bother,
it seems as though you never
loved a single bit of me.
But here I am stuck in your world,
pondering why I should even bother,
and oh darling I have done what
you told—all of them;
for you to know I love you.
But now, why do I even bother,
you're a poison I can never let go.

Veritas

It is you that I need always
for I can breathe the air as you do—
drink the water as you do.
This anguish I bear because you
seeped out of my life—
for that I will remain close to you.
But comes a day you will fall in love—
not with me.
And I will endure to live;
even if it is you I desire always.
Loving you was not meant to be;
like a two-edged sword,
it hurts to love someone like you.

Lie To Me

To hear it from you
and may it reach the angels, too.
Three words that can set me free
and away from a love's demise.
The devils have been lingering
in my thoughts for too long
and I cannot suffer in your Hell any longer.
Please just lie to me and tell me this is something—
I suffered way too long and your fictitious love is the only cure.
To lose a person was never my choice;
a crucial sacrifice in my desires to regret—
it was you I was never meant to forget.

Embrace

To fall again from grace,
it is your presence I can only desire.
A strode along this wintry way
you have left behind,
has the Sun been with you—
all I can ask for is your summer warmth.
Though within your embrace,
I can never truly trust.
Because all the while,
we conceal our faces;
cowering our true colors amidst
our "I missed you" embrace.

Her Whiskey

You love me
but you tell me to go.
I stay and you tell me to move on.
You held on tight,
two arms clenched around me—
said, "don't you ever leave or
else the world will fall on me."
Here I stayed in promise to never hurt,
clung my hand onto yours
and had you in my grasp.
I kissed you fairy tales
until your world was bright.
But forever came today;
you cried and chose not to love—
two heavenly hearts I hoped was certain from above.

His White Tulip

I planted you a garden,
a field full of flowers,
in hopes that these seeds could hold
the roots of our august romance.
Without hesitation, without regret,
I told you promises in hopes
to fly you away and we'll be
like the petals of autumn floating in air.
Yet we went separate ways,
and these flowers have lost their colour.
It has been past winter yet it is still cold,
the Heavens have been crying...
...enough tears to water a white tulip.

Empty Spaces

There are many days I want to say hello,
and ask how your day went like how I used to.
But sometimes I need to step back and see for myself,
how much I took you for granted.
Now there are countless nights that end up in haze,
asking myself how you are nowadays.
Because in this void, there are empty spaces
I need to get accustomed to—
having no clue how you filled these spaces
and left me feeling brand new.

Cupid

Cupid, my friend, is it over?
Have I failed to conceal a forever?
You gave me a chance to love her—
God, she was a true treasure.
We fell in love again together
though blinded by the love you offered.
Thus at the moment of my failure,
she was gone like breath caught on a mirror.

A Broken Promise

You did not come.
The flowers have torn apart.
May not be I lose you.
I am forever waiting for you.
You did not come.

Do you love me?
You love not me.
Thus be not the soul of mine—
you dearly passion.
With the veins within me—
you not unite.
Forever together,
I will try.
Do you love me?

Farewell, my angel.
Time is past.
Pained soul I once possessed—
had slowly arise from me.
A broken heart within me,
I, you do not love—
farewell, my angel.

Falling Away

There she goes
falling in love with another man.
Wait, wait, wait,
I need to catch a breath.
I cannot run fast—
you move on too fast.

Wait, wait, wait,
an emotion!
A laughing matter I suppose.
You smile and I cry,
you turn my hellos into goodbyes.

If losing you makes me wonder
were we really lovers that didn't make it?
Like fallen angels?—
"If losing you makes you happy,
why does it make me cry?"

Ifs & Whats

If I was yours,
can the whole world doubt
what we have?
When I fall in your scaffolds,
and dwindle down your heart—
catch me and darling, I will be yours.

If you claim me,
will you be proud to call me yours?—
And when we wake up,
can you promise that I will get to see
your drowsy-self smile in the mornings?

All I ask is for a reassurance—
if time took its course,
and when you leave,
will I still be the happy man you admired?

Will You Always Be There

Under the shadow,
we held our hands in promise
that we could last forever.
Now alone and under an umbrella,
this crying sky weeps for
the Sun to shine again.

The clouds so dreary in a day so weary...
...I'm missing you dearly.
On my knees with my hands on praying,
I pray to God every day to look after you
like I promised in our saddest goodbye.

To Face the Raven

It is true—I'm so blue.
Sweet melody where hath been thyself?
Leave me in angst while you change your ocean's tide.
May it be quick and abrupt,
the ravens fly unto me to corrupt this dying heart.

You Let Me Go

I am not ignoring you,
I am afraid of you.
You let go and parted ways,
you left every piece of me crumbling—
placing me into a void where
your sins have been hiding all along.

I Let You Go

Farewell the blue sky
and the yellow sun.
The red moon gently serenades
this crying, empty soul.
I yearn to break your seal
and let my heart rest from your sins.
My angels will listen and I will be saved—
they will mend the depths of your hell from scarring.
I pray to let go in silence,
to be gone with our love's demise
will be my salvation.

A. P. A. L. A. C. E.

M. A. D. E.

O. F. J. A. D. E.

As I write this last chapter,

I run out of ink and

these unwritten words

will perish and will only live

until my heart forgets.

VII

Why I Write

I write because it unravels my mind,
slowly soothing the sorrow in my soul,
allowing me to dig deep down—
healing my harrowed heart.
Thus I pursuit my prize:
just jubilance—
like the one from yesterday.

Lost in Memories

Let us wander around in this hopeless palace;
dare we not escape and stay in love for a lifetime.
Let daylight end, more stars will gleam for us to dance.
Thus we will be lost in our memories—
holding onto our pasts until they all swift away.

Follow River

Dearest, take my sins away—
away from grief that stole my course.
I have been following the rivers
until the light dismays.
Thus lead my way to pursuit a purpose;
have I thought of things that led me astray—
following the rivers until the light swifts away.

River Falls

Where the river ends
the storm seeks of serenity.
Ripples and tidal waves flow through Gaia
and this rain has left a sky
a crescent covered in colors.

River Ripples

Rivers rippled violently and
so did the heartbeat of mine.
You said our love hindered
when everything was just fine.

Laying upon enchanted grounds,
your love never went unnoticed—
o' how could you be so heartless?

I never intended to let go.
And now I cower to look back—
our fondest memories would break my heart.

Lost in Translation

She appeared in my dreams
even though I was vexed
from her within.
She despised the thought
of loving me
though in my dream
our love was rekindling.
I woke up feeling relieved,
only to find out—
it was only just a dream.
I was lost in translation,
lingering in the past ruefully.

Lovely Ways

In her eyes I was her dream;
seeing her looking at me as if the whole universe
was in her grasp.
Now I'm the beast;
in her eyes I purge nothing but anger and hatred.
Burning the lovely ways that we went through,
two hearts that collided...
...ended up subsiding.

A Saying About Love

Love is a dominion—
an agonizing and astonishing
double-entendre.
Both can accentuate into such
deep measures of being loved
and being hurt by the ugliness
of such beautiful entity.

Foolish Love

Forever was a long time
for the two of us.
We were too innocent,
young and daft.
We fooled our hearts
and built ourselves a sandcastle
only to disappear once upon a time.

Circus Girl

There I was, amidst the crowd,
seemingly searching for some sort of love.
I flushed a smile so endearingly across my face.
But I got lost in the crowd before
I fell in love with the circus girl.

Pages

I got an
empty paper
and a pen
full of ink.
Blank pages
Ready for a
Scrawl
And all I could
write about
is you.

Seven Seas

The cold water rippling beneath our feet
as we dance across the bluest ocean.
Long walks by a California beach—
it is with your hand on mine that I truly desire.
Dancing across the Seven Seas—
I will never tire until death sets us apart.

But A Fairy Tale

They were young, they were free,
they were in love in the reasons
the whole world could understand.
Though when asked about
their loved story, she replied,
"We were but a fairy tale."

A Life in Fairytale

Never live in a fairytale—
you'll cry in the evening.
By morning when the sun comes up,
your tears will dry
and soon again,
you will wear your crown.
Dripping in fantasy
and melting your reality
into nothingness once again.

Death

Death, do me of ways
I have never done before.
Quoth you, Death,
"I've found a way."
And the angels have come,
and unto me I am gone,
and "I've found a way," you said.

A Great Pretender

A face behind the mask is seen—
no immaculate illation cannot bear
such problems within.
"A pretentious mask," the man declared,—
can a lie be worn...
Many faces to please the pleaser —
a great pretender.

Her Ways

Has she lost her way?
Never to be found again.
Lost in darkness—
never to see the light and
witness the celestial beauty
of what was once hers.
"Soothe me as I seek my old ways,
away from this nightmare,
a painless poison it is,
I suppose," she said.

Her Soul

Here, her soul
sing of sorrows.
Hear her sing
a song of adoration
and her tears fill
the emptiness inside—
succumbing to her valiant heart.

The Glittery Box

99 dates and our memories written in a box;
to each contained promises and wishes
for two lovers in their newfound love.
The angels sang their carols as we spent
our eve of love and laughs.
Though to give away and let it go,
Four Christmases spent in wonderland
yet we have dismayed our glow.
We dreamt too soon and nothing came anew—
Every Christmas is last Christmas
and we broke away too soon.

Shelled In

It is easy to say I won't bear
your burdens anymore—
to leave you be
and not give a damn about you.
It is easy to say I don't care about you—
but to act upon it kills me every single day.
But all is fine, don't you worry.
I still love you like
how the moon admires the morning sun.

Painted Heart

She painted with words
and used her tears
to remind her how much she was hurt.
Her heart was empty—
a blank canvas waiting to be painted on.
As the days passed by,
she wished for a prince to paint her away—
to draw her out of the blue
and brush away the emptiness in her heart.

Vale

If she is happy,
then let her be.
I do not want to stand
in happiness' way
if the rain persists to
rain only on me.
For life became more poetic
when she said goodbye.

A Palace Made of Jade

All good things can always come to an end.
These memories will always hold onto
something worth beyond happiness...

...like a palace made of jade, our memory houses
the good times and it let us heal through
the warm happiness of our lives.

*-dearpoet_*